My May 9-12, 2008 Vacation with
Donna + Walt, Boulder, Colorado
(they bought this book for me)

Boulder's
Favorite Places

Photography and Text by
Russell and Gail Dohrmann

Colorado Littlebooks

WESTCLIFFE PUBLISHERS
westcliffepublishers.com

Introduction

Visitors to Boulder, Colorado, usually approach the city from the east along US Highway 36. As the highway reaches the apex of Davidson Mesa, those who stop at the viewpoint can see the Boulder Valley and the city of Boulder spread out below. To the west are two mountain ranges: the foothills just west of Boulder, containing the Flatiron formations of Green Mountain and Bear Peak, and the frequently snow-capped Indian Peaks of the Rocky Mountains along the Continental Divide. Marshall Mesa forms the southern border of the valley, while to the north, the foothills range all the way to the edge of Rocky Mountain National Park, where Longs Peak is visible on most days. Almost straight ahead, the red rooftops of the University of Colorado direct visitors to the architecturally renowned campus, aptly located in the heart of Boulder.

Boulder was established as a gold mining camp in 1858 with the construction of the first log cabins at the mouth of Boulder Canyon. After incorporation in 1871, the city continued to grow—the University of Colorado opened its first building, Old Main, in 1877, and by 1890 the population had reached 4,000. Growth controls for the city were instituted in the 1970s, and today the population hovers around 100,000. Seventy percent of Boulder residents are under the age of 44, including nearly 30,000 college students.

Boulder's opportunities for recreation are enhanced by the area's natural beauty. Boulder Creek flows from the mouth of Boulder Canyon between Flagstaff Mountain and the unique redrock hogback formations of Settlers Park. Early on, the City of Boulder recognized this unique environment and established the Open Space and Mountain Parks Department to protect the beauty and habitat of the mountains west of the city and to provide extensive natural areas for recreation. Currently, over 200 miles of hiking and biking trails crisscross Boulder's plains and foothills. In addition to the beauty of the city's natural setting, over 300 sunny days annually (more than San Diego!) keep Boulder residents constantly engaged in recreational activities all year long. The most visited natural area is Chautauqua Park at the base of the Flatirons. With its grassy meadow, historic dining hall and auditorium, and starting points for trails, Chautauqua offers visitors much to enjoy. The nearby road winds to the summit of Flagstaff Mountain, passing Panorama Point's views of the city and Boulder Valley and reaching a picnic area and Sunrise Circle Amphitheater at the summit.

Over 25 years ago, the downtown area of Boulder was converted to a pedestrian mall by bricking in the streets and planting trees, grass, shrubs, and flowers. To this day, extensive landscaping and many shopping and dining amenities invite Boulderites and visitors to enjoy street performers and the festivals that regularly occur at the mall. By providing activities that all can share, the mall helps maintain a small-town feel and a sense of community rare in a city this size.

Boulder is a special place with a unique personality—it's known nationally for its beauty, its youthful love of recreation, its spirited politics and forward thinking, and its casual style. After living in Boulder for over 30 years, we have attempted to portray our love for Boulder through photographs of the place we hope to always call home.

—Gail and Russell Dohrmann

Downtown

In 1977, the Pearl Street Mall was established by bricking in the streets and creating decorative flowerbeds and planters. Tulips of many varieties bloom each year in April and are replaced by leafy plants and flowers throughout the summer.

Hearts on a Swing, a bronze sculpture by George Lundeen, welcomes visitors to the Pearl Street Mall on the east side of Broadway.

To the delight of young children and their parents, a renovation of the Pearl Street Mall in 2002 added a pop-jet fountain near the 14th Street crossing.

One Boulder Plaza provides mixed-use commercial, office, and residential space in downtown Boulder. In the winter, a skating rink operates in the courtyard.

The Boulder Theater on 14th Street first opened in 1936. It was designed in the Art Deco style to complement the courthouse that was built across the street a few years before.

Illuminated by holiday lights and a colorful sunset, the Boulder Cafe sits at the corner of 13th Street and the Pearl Street Mall. The restaurant occupies the original Boulder National Bank building, built in the late 19th century.

Constructed in 1933 in the Art Deco style, the Boulder County Courthouse replaced an older Victorian structure that was destroyed by fire. The Lions Club fountain was built and placed in the plaza in 1935, and was restored to use in 1998 with funding from the Lions Club of Boulder.

During a visit to Boulder in 1987, the mayor of Dushanbe, Tajikistan, offered a gift to the city: a teahouse hand-carved and hand-painted by artisans of Tajikistan. The Boulder Dushanbe Teahouse was erected at its present site on 13th Street between Canyon and Arapahoe, and opened with a celebration in May 1998.

Plentiful antique roses highlight the decorative motif on the front facade of the Boulder Dushanbe Teahouse. Carved ceilings and columns adorn the unique interior.

The garden of the newly constructed St. Julien Hotel affords a nice view of the Flatirons to the south. The hotel opened in 2005, but was named after a historic Boulder hotel that operated from 1898–1923.

The oldest operating hotel in Boulder, and a nationally registered landmark, the Hotel Boulderado opened on New Year's Day in 1909. The name is a combination of "Boulder" and "Colorado." It is known for its stunningly extravagant stained glass ceiling, which rises up high above the lobby.

In 1992, an expansion and renovation of the original Boulder Public Library was completed, with a bridge across Boulder Creek to a new main section. Architect Alan Stromberg had existing areas refitted to create an auditorium and gallery.

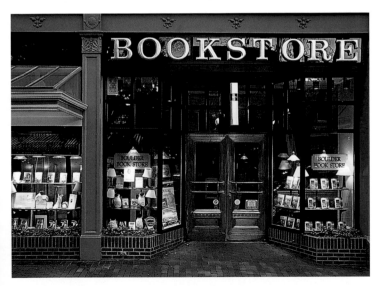

A Pearl Street Mall mainstay, the independently owned Boulder Bookstore opened in 1973. On its four floors, the store has at least 100,000 titles available for sale at any one time.

Boulder Creek flows through Eben G. Fine Park at 4th Street, at the mouth of Boulder Canyon on the western edge of town. One of the oldest parks in Boulder, it was named for the secretary of the Boulder Chamber of Commerce from 1927–1935.

The Evert Pierson Kids' Fishing Ponds are stocked with fish during the summer months, and in the fall, the maples that surround the ponds turn shades of red and gold. A kids' fishing derby is one of the events held here during the annual Boulder Creek Fest.

The Arnett-Fullen House was built at the corner of 7th Street and Pearl in 1877, and it stands today as an especially fine example of Victorian "gingerbread" and wrought-iron craftsmanship.

Broadway Bridge crosses Boulder Creek and provides pedestrian underpasses for bicycling, walking, and jogging. This reconstructed bridge replaced the older version in 2004.

Nicknamed the "Mork & Mindy" house, as its exteriors were used in the popular television show of the same name in the 1970s and '80s, this Victorian house has been as well maintained as many of Boulder's other historic homes.

Naropa University 2130

Lincoln School, built in 1903, now houses Naropa University, a Buddhist-founded liberal arts college that offers ten graduate programs and eight undergraduate degree programs in fields such as education, environmentalism, and religious studies.

University of Colorado

Colorful fall trees frame the original library building at the University of Colorado. Opened in 1904, it was Boulder's first library building, replacing the one room in Old Main that served as the library. Having undergone several renovations in keeping with its original style, the building now houses the Department of Theater and Dance.

Hale Science Building was named for Horace Hale, the second president of the university, and now houses the Department of Anthropology. A good example of Richardsonian Romanesque architecture, the stone building is over 100 years old.

In 1909, construction began on Macky Auditorium; it was finally completed in 1922. A noted example of Collegiate Gothic style, the auditorium currently seats 2,047 people after a renovation in 1986. Macky Auditorium is used for community and university events.

Situated on the northeast corner of Norlin Quadrangle, Eaton Humanities is the newest building on the quad. Dedicated in November 1999, it was named to honor Woody and Leslie Eaton, whose contribution went toward instructional technology for the building.

Old Main was the first and only building on the University of Colorado campus when it began operating in 1877. Still in use today, it houses a chapel and the Heritage Center, which celebrates the history of the university.

Named for F. G. Folsom, a revered University of Colorado football coach in the 1940s, newly renovated Folsom Stadium towers over the campus. Not only is the stadium the venue for Colorado Buffaloes football, it also hosts graduation, Fourth of July fireworks, and the annual Bolder Boulder race.

Cicero's words, "Who knows only his own generation remains always a child," comprise the inscription for Norlin Library, named for former CU president George Norlin. The building, situated on the east side of Norlin Quadrangle, is the state's largest academic library.

Just across the street from the campus, The Hill is a lively shopping district that features restaurants and entertainment venues. The Sink, established in 1923, is a well-loved hangout for students.

Buchanan's Coffee Pub, at the corner of 13th Street and College Avenue, provides an off-campus center for studying, latté-drinking, and socializing.

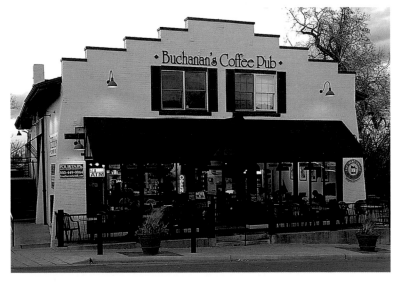

Varsity Bridge, which spans Varsity Lake, is a favorite campus rendezvous. It is especially lovely in the fall, when the golden trees surrounding the lake reflect in the water.

Chautauqua

The porch of the Chautauqua Dining Hall is a premium spot for dinner during summer months. A restaurant now operates the facility, which has had many culinary incarnations since its inception in 1898.

Magenta bee balm blooms on Enchanted Mesa. This scenic foothills view also includes Chautauqua Auditorium, which was built in 1898 by the Colorado-Texas Chautauqua Association.

In spring, winter snows
in Chautauqua Meadow
give way to a carpet of
green grass sprinkled with
dramatic wildflowers such
as arnica, wild iris, and
silver lupine.

The Mesa Trail begins at Chautauqua Meadow above Chautauqua Park and winds south 6 miles, terminating near Eldorado Springs. The trail has become a favorite of local hikers and runners.

Flagstaff Mountain

Built during the Great Depression by the Civilian Conservation Corps, the Flagstaff Mountain Sunrise Circle Amphitheater still serves the community as a popular site for weddings, gatherings, retirement ceremonies, and an annual Easter sunrise service. The amphitheater was restored in 2004.

Hikes

In the fall, the sumac along the South Boulder Creek Trail turns a brilliant red.

In North Boulder, a network of trails up Mount Sanitas is very popular, especially with local residents, who often hike here on a daily basis. The profile of the distinctive Dakota Ridge is visible from downtown and from Flagstaff Mountain.

Boulder's climate is semi-arid, with an average rainfall of only 18 inches. Fog is very infrequent. Drenching spring showers and cool temperatures allowed for this rare moment on the Ute–Range View Trail.

Royal Arch, a natural redrock formation on Green Mountain, is accessible by a strenuous hike that originates at the Chautauqua ranger's cottage and gains 1,320 vertical feet over 1.4 miles. From this vantage point, the entire Boulder Valley can be seen to the east.

One of the area's natural wonders, Boulder Falls splashes in Boulder Canyon 11 miles west of Boulder. Thunderous in the spring, the falls' gushing water tapers off in the fall.

Famous for its steep-walled canyon and technical climbing routes, Eldorado State Park south of Boulder is a mecca for rock climbers and hikers throughout the region.

Farms and Ranches

Boulder's rural origins are evident on the eastern edge of town, where farms and ranches mix with suburban living. Cattle are still raised and pastured here in protected open space.

Hay is raised and harvested several times per year along South Boulder Road, just east of the city.

Historic Harf Barn, an unoccupied structure located on Boulder County open space, is framed by rime-frosted cottonwoods and waist-high dried grasses and weeds.

Several scenic old barns dot the rural landscape east of Boulder, providing a pleasant contrast to the sophisticated urban areas of town. Some of these barns are still in use today.

This ranch on the south end of Boulder on Highway 93 still raises cattle. In the fall, cloudless blue skies contrast with the season's golden hues.

Lakes

Opportunities for hiking, photography, fishing, and picnicking abound at Sawhill Ponds. Its 18 individual ponds and wildlife preserve are the result of a gravel mining reclamation project.

Wonderland Lake is located on the Dakota hogback in North Boulder. The area attracts hikers, bikers, and other recreationists. Protected areas are home to rare grasses and plants, including needle-and-thread grass, Bell's twin pod, and New Mexican feather grass.

Boulder Reservoir has numerous recreational uses in addition to providing part of Boulder's water supply. Along with water-skiing, swimming, boating, and picnicking, the Kinetic Sculpture Challenge is held here each spring, and several triathlons take place during the summer months.

Mesa Reservoir was created by the Silver Lake Ditch Company to provide irrigation for farms in the region, but was soon supplanted by other reservoirs. Hiking trails now crisscross the territory.

Especially scenic at sunrise and sunset, Coot Lake is just north of the Boulder Reservoir pumping station. The trail around the lake is a short 1.2-mile walk that connects to other trails at the reservoir.

Sports

Boulder Reservoir provides the perfect venue for the swimming leg of a triathlon, several of which are held each year in Boulder.

Boulder has had a great fondness for bicycle racing and racers ever since 1975, when the Red Zinger Bicycle Classic began in North Boulder Park. The Morgul-Bismarck loop in south Boulder County is a classic, grueling ride that features the infamous "wall," a sharp 1-mile stretch that becomes increasingly steeper.

Racers compete in the North Boulder Park Criterium, a race with a specified number of laps around a relatively short course featuring sharp corners and straightaways. Men and women vie for premiums on individual laps as well as an overall win.

Held every Memorial Day since 1979, the Bolder Boulder is a 10k race for elite runners, citizen runners, and walkers. It originates at the First National Bank of Colorado at 30th Street and the Diagonal Highway and ends at the University of Colorado's Folsom Stadium. Over 45,000 participants take part in the race annually.

The aptly named Pleasant View Soccer Fields, near the Diagonal Highway, provide athletes of all ages with a place to play from spring until the fall months.

Shallow, relatively calm areas on Boulder Creek give way to whitewater below Eben G. Fine Park, attracting kayakers of all skill levels.

In the spring, daredevil tubers appreciate the rushing water in Boulder Creek, created by heavy runoff from melting mountain snow. The flow tapers off to a more moderate stream in early summer, attracting tubers who just want to beat the heat.

An ice climber in Boulder Canyon performs a technical climb, ice axe in hand. Boulder's rocky slopes, youthful enthusiasts, and good weather make climbing one of the most popular recreational activities in the region. Eldorado Canyon alone has over 500 documented climbing routes.

Festivals and Events

In one of Boulder's wackiest traditions, contestants in the Kinetic Sculpture Challenge at the Boulder Reservoir celebrate the end of winter with a parade on Pearl Street Mall.

The Kinetics race requires a team of costumed individuals to race their home-constructed vehicles across land and water and through thick mud. "Aesthetics" also count in this entertaining race.

The Boulder Farmers' Market offers local produce grown on small farms, much of it organic, to residents at informal markets. Often supplemented by craft sales and food booths, these tantalizing markets happen twice a week from mid-April through mid-October.

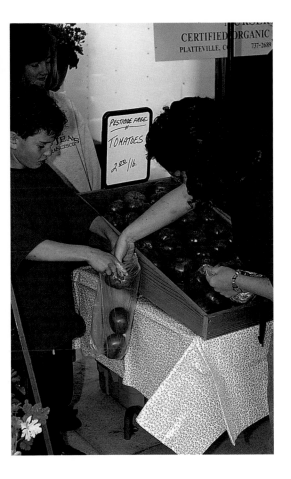

NCAR

Perched on top of a mesa below Boulder's Flatirons, NCAR (the National Center for Atmospheric Research) is a landmark for the city. Its angular concrete planes, the color of sandstone, were designed by I. M. Pei to be compatible with the center's surroundings.

High Schools

"Minnie" and "Jake," the Art Deco sculptures over the entrance to Boulder High School, created a bit of controversy when they were completed in 1937, although the mascots were said to represent "wisdom" and "strength."

As the population grew in south Boulder, a second high school became necessary. Fairview High School, situated on a bluff above Viele Lake, opened in 1971, and has since added a new 14,000-square-foot library and updated science classrooms.

Wildlife

A wide variety of wildlife exists in and around the Boulder city limits. The most numerous of these animals include deer, coyotes, geese, ducks, songbirds, raccoons, and squirrels. Several bears and even some mountain lions

have been spotted in the foothills in recent years. Since it is surrounded by unincorporated land, Boulder has had a large deer population in its residential areas for many years. Usually a herd of deer can be seen in the meadow below NCAR. And—love them or hate them —prairie dogs have almost totemic significance for Boulderites. These cute little rascals have incited much controversy over the years as people encroach upon their habitat.

ISBN-10: 1-56579-534-2
ISBN-13: 978-1-56579-534-1

Photography and text copyright: Russell and Gail Dohrmann, 2006. All rights reserved.

Editor: Barrett Webb
Graphic Design: Beckie Smith, www.BeckieArt.com
Production Manager: Craig Keyzer

Published by:
Westcliffe Publishers, Inc.
P.O. Box 1261
Englewood, CO 80150

Printed in China by: C&C Offset Printing Co., Ltd.

Library of Congress Cataloging-in-Publication Data:
Dohrmann, Russell.
   Boulder's favorite places / text and photography by Russell and Gail Dohrmann.
       p. cm.
   ISBN-13: 978-1-56579-534-1
   ISBN-10: 1-56579-534-2
 1.   Boulder (Colo.)--Pictorial works.   2.   Historic sites--Colorado--Boulder--Pictorial works.
3.   Historic buildings--Colorado--Boulder--Pictorial works.   4.   Boulder (Colo.)--Buildings,
structures, etc.--Pictorial works.   I. Dohrmann, Gail. II. Title.
   F784.B66D64 2006
   978.8'6300222--dc22   2006008600

*For more information about other fine books and calendars from Westcliffe Publishers, please contact your local bookstore, call us at 1-800-523-3692, or visit us on the Web at **westcliffepublishers.com**.*

About the Photographers

Longtime Boulder residents Russell and Gail Dohrmann are avid photographers. Their favorite photographic interests range from travel to scenic, romantic, and creative subjects, as well as flowers and still life. They enjoy combining their photography with their outdoor activities: hiking, fitness walking, snowshoeing,

and bicycling. After attending the University of Colorado in the 1960s, they have been Boulder residents since 1971 and have seen many of the city's changes over the years, such as the creation of the Pearl Street Mall—now one of the focal points of Boulder life. With all the beauty that surrounds Boulder, it is no wonder they have been inspired to try to capture on film the unique aspects of the city and its surroundings.

Russell and Gail are members of several Colorado arts and photography organizations including the Boulder Art Association and Flatirons Photography Club. Their work has been published in magazines, calendars, cards, and books. Most recently, they were the photographers for *Best Boulder Region Hiking Trails,* published by Westcliffe Publishers in 2005.

A photo essay on fall in Colorado appeared in *Country Magazine.* They also exhibit their print photography at local and regional photography and art shows, where they have been recognized for their work.